unloved

Michael A. Pender Sr.

THE BROOK PUBLISHING COMPANY

HOUSTON

Copyright © 2015 by Michael A. Pender, Sr.

All rights reserved. This book or any portion thereof may not be reproduced or used in any manner whatsoever without the express written permission of the publisher except for the use of brief quotations in a book review.

ISBN 978-0-692-42871-9

The Brook Publishing Company
Fallbrook Church
12512 Walters Road
Houston, TX 77014
www.fallbrookchurch.org

Unless otherwise indicated, all Scripture quotations are taken from the New American Standard Version of the Bible, copyright © 1960, 1962, 1963, 1968, 1971, 1972, 1973, 1975, 1977, 1995 by The Lockman Foundation. Used by permission. (www.Lockman.org)

Printed in the United States of America

unloved

Table of Contents

Foreword

•7•

Acknowledgements

•11•

Introduction

•13•

"Unloved," Leah's Song of Sorrow

•17•

CHAPTER 1: *The Tale of Two Sisters*

•19•

CHAPTER 2: *The Reality of Leah's Unloved Condition*

•29•

CHAPTER 3: *Leah's Recognition and Reaction to Her Unloved Condition*

•41•

Chapter 4: *God's View of Unloved Life in the Womb*

•59•

Chapter 5: *Jacob, You're Going to Love Me*

•75•

Chapter 6: *Leah Finds Peace*

•85•

Chapter 7: *God, You Will Always Love Me*

•91•

"My Beloved," Leah's Song of Peace

•97•

Endnotes

•99•

About the Author

•101•

foreword

I AM HONORED TO WRITE THIS FOREWORD FOR MY husband. This year, we celebrated twenty-seven years of marriage. It has been a blessed journey of laughter, tears, but most of all…love.

Our love story began in the spring of 1985, at church, while working together in the Bus Ministry. I thought Michael was mighty cute, and I was so nervous to talk to him. But God worked on my courage, and we soon became friends. We talked on the phone daily for hours, and each Saturday we would minister together by visiting individuals on our bus route. During those few years, I witnessed firsthand my husband's love for God and his integrity to live by His Word.

It was exhilarating! I was a sold-out Christian, and now I had met someone with the same passion. In our time of talking, sharing, and studying each other, we quickly moved from friends to "I really care for this person." However, three magic words my husband unexpectedly spilled out to me sealed my heart forever. These are three most important, life-changing words that touches a deep tender cord in every human being's heart: "I love you."

My heart was set ablaze! Immediately I had a renewed sense of purpose and longing. Within my being, I knew I loved Michael, but I hadn't been so sure about his feelings. God confirmed Michael's love for me in a magnificent way, and three years later we became one in marriage.

With great hesitation I share my love story. I realize there are many women whose relationships are painful. However, I've come to appreciate my love story as a testimony of God's grace and blessing. I don't deserve my husband's love, but God allows me to experience it and to know it in a special way. For this, I'm grateful.

God's purpose is for every person to experience genuine, sacrificial love from another. His Word is filled with the mandate to love: *"Beloved, let us love one another, for love is of God...* (1 John

4:7); *"A new commandment I give to you, that you love one another; as I have loved you…"* (John 13:34); *"Love suffers long and is kind…love never fails…and now abide faith, hope, love, these three, but the greatest of these is love"* (1 Corinthians 13:4, 8, 13). Love is important to God, and He has given us the capacity to give it and receive it.

Undoubtedly, Michael realizes there are many who are not giving love to others and many more who are not receiving genuine love. Because this is a reality for countless women, God has entrusted my pastor-husband with the message of this book.

Michael longs for the unloved woman to know that there is a God who sees, understands, and is fighting for her to feel worthy of love. He longs for the unloved woman to know how to cry out to God, how to watch for His deliverance, and how to praise Him in the midst of it all. My husband's heart is set on teaching God's truth: that every individual, whether male or female, is loved fiercely by our God.

I know this book will accomplish its intended

purpose. It has helped me to understand the length God will go to in order to fight for those who are His. As you journey through this book, allow your heart to open, to be unhindered, so that God has room to fill it with His pure love.

Janice Pender

acknowledgements

THIS BOOK IS DEDICATED TO THE MIGHTY WOMEN of Fallbrook Church—First to my wife, the love of my life, Janice, whose undying commitment to my calling, baffles me even today. Our love gives me the liberty to minister without reservation to women who are hurting. You inspire me to encourage them to live up to their God potential because of what I get to witness every morning when I wake up to your beautiful smile. To my mother, Mrs. Lila Pender, we don't get to choose our parents, but if we did, I would choose you. Your unconditional love has carried me through the rough streets of the Bronx, into the hallowed pulpit of Fallbrook Church and for that I will be eternally grateful. And finally to the women of Fallbrook, the backbone of this ministry, you too have been my creative muse for what the reader will find in the pages of this book. Your uncompromised reverence of God reminds me of this scripture in Proverbs 31:29 -30:

"Many women do noble things, but you surpass them all. Charm is deceptive, and beauty is fleeting; but a woman who fears the Lord is to be praised."

I salute you for your diligence in serving and seeking God. I feel honored to have a front row seat to witness God's handiwork in your lives.

Forever Grateful.

Michael A. Pender
Son, Husband and Pastor

introduction

WE ARE ABOUT TO EMBARK ON A JOURNEY INTO AN area that is often neglected, though everyone has or will experience this at least once in their lives in some form or other.

Being "unloved" has become a norm in our present day society. This condition is a threat to one's personal stability and plays a major role in many of the ills in our society, from substance abuse, mental illness, and the ever-increasing number of single parents in America today. The root cause of most of these atrocities is that these individuals were not loved by their original caregivers, or not now loved by their mates.

It has become commonplace in our nation to disregard people because we don't perceive their value. But God does. He looks at the *heart* of an individual instead their outward appearance.

Throughout history there has been no other people group more exploited than women. Some say that the cause of this goes back to the Garden of Eden and lies at the feet of the mother of all humanity, Eve. In her decision to willfully partake of the forbidden fruit when urged by the tempter, she brought this curse on all womankind. In Genesis 3:16, God told the woman because of her sin,

> *I will greatly multiply your sorrow and your conception;*
> *In pain you shall bring forth children;*
> *Your desire shall be for your husband,*
> *And he shall rule over you.*

The unprecedented number of single mothers in our communities today is, in many ways, connected to the exploitation of women in our society. In no way is that an excuse for irresponsible behavior by any group of people in our civilization; however, in light of the current crisis we share, there are issues that need to be addressed in order for productive change to take place.

In this book, you will discover that being unloved is a condition that should not be made light of. It's not a figment of one's imagination. And it's not a place in which you must or need to remain.

Using the story of Leah, Jacob's wife, as our backdrop, we will deal with this great threat to personal stability and learn just how compassionately and wholly God Himself loves us. Join us as we explore how God ministers to those who are unloved…including *you*.

"UNLOVED"

LEAH'S SONG OF SORROW

My heart weeps for a love that it has been denied for years.
I find solace in his arms when he speaks kind words to me
in the early hours of the morning,
But, well, he's never said the words that my hungry heart
wants to hear.
Those words are, "I love you."
I've given him three children; sons are the fruit of my womb.
And she...well, she's given him none.
But I see the way he looks at her, and my soul cries out for
a fraction of the tenderness he freely gives to her.
If only God would turn his heart to me, if only he could see
that I possess so much more than she does...
Beauty isn't everything.
My unrequited love haunts me in the midnight hour when
he is with her and I embrace my pillow,
Sobbing in remembrance of our last time together.

MICHAEL A. PENDER

> *He holds my heart in his hand like a callous toy,*
> *He abuses it and denies it the very thing that would bring it joy.*
> *My sorrow is compounded with the truth of my private guilt...*
> *I deceived him, and this is my punishment,*
> *Living a loveless life forever.*

chapter 1
THE TALE OF TWO SISTERS

Somebody will always be unloved.

OUR STORY, THE "TALE OF TWO SISTERS," starts with a love triangle. The point on the triangle are Jacob son of Isaac, and Rachel and Leah, daughters of Laban. The story unfolds in Genesis 29:16-35.

Now Laban had two daughters; the name of the older was Leah, and the name of the younger was Rachel. And Leah's eyes were weak, but Rachel was beautiful of form and face. Now Jacob loved Rachel, so he said, "I will serve you seven years for your younger daughter Rachel." Laban said, "It is better that I give her to you than to give her to another man; stay with me." So Jacob served seven years for Rachel and they seemed to him but a few days because of his love for her.

Then Jacob said to Laban, "Give me my wife, for my time is completed, that I may go in to her." Laban gathered all the men of the place and made a feast. Now in the evening he took his daughter Leah, and brought her to him, and Jacob went in to her. Laban also gave his maid Zilpah to his daughter Leah as a maid. So it came about in the morning that, behold, it was Leah! And he said to Laban, "What is this you have done to me? Was it not for Rachel that I served with you? Why then have you deceived me?" But Laban said, "It is not the practice in our place to marry off the younger before the firstborn. Complete the week of this one, and we will give you the other also for the service which you shall serve with me for another seven years." Jacob did so and completed her week, and he gave him his daughter Rachel as his wife. Laban also gave his maid Bilhah to his daughter Rachel as her maid. So Jacob went in to Rachel also, and indeed he loved Rachel more than Leah, and he served with Laban for another seven years.

> *Now the LORD saw that Leah was unloved, and He opened her womb, but Rachel was barren. Leah conceived and bore a son and named him Reuben, for she said, "Because the LORD has seen my affliction; surely now my husband will love me." Then she conceived again and bore a son and said, "Because the LORD has heard that I am un-loved, He has given me this son also." So she named him Simeon. She conceived again and bore a son and said, "Now this time my husband will become attached to me because I have borne him three sons." Therefore he was named Levi. And she conceived again and bore a son and said, "This time I will praise the LORD." Therefore she named him Judah. Then she stopped bearing.*

It is a tragic tale. But there is much we can learn from it. Let's start with the male lead of this story, Jacob.

Even in the very midst of his entry into this world, Jacob was fighting for position. His very name means "supplanter." He grabbed the heel of his brother to get out of the womb first. He lied to his father to get the birthright of the firstborn. He then had to run away from home because his brother threatened to kill him for his deception and theft. He ended up residing in a foreign land as a servant at the home of his uncle.

There, he fell in love with his uncle's youngest daughter. He agreed to work for her for seven years, and the Scripture says it was his pleasure to work for her because of how much he loved her.

Jacob was a man of extreme determination. If he wanted something, it was obvious that he would go to great lengths to get what he wanted. He betrayed his brother and lied to his father for the firstborn birthright, so working seven years for the woman he fell in love with at first sight would seem like "days to him."

But his earlier actions opened the door for deception to come to him, Laban being the tool that the tempter used to bring about retribution. When the switch was made on his wedding day and the marriage consummated on the wedding night, Jacob was stuck married to a woman he did not love. Imagine a young man's anticipation of a night with his beloved after working for her for seven years, and then finding out the next morning that she had escaped him!

Leah bore Jacob's initial wrath after the deception, and would bear the cross for her father's duplicity for the rest of her life.

But though her husband regarded her as unlovely, *God* declared that Leah was worthy. He becomes the Father or Husband that is unavailable in relationships. His love never changes and is readily available wherever and whenever we need it. He has a purpose for each of us…and Leah's life was not without purpose.

She bore Jacob six sons and a daughter, Levi and Judah coming from the fruit of her womb. From the tribe of Levi came the priests of God, and from Judah came King David. In David's ancestry came Jesus Christ Himself. And, according to Tamar Kadari in her discussion entitled "Leah: Midrash and Aggadah," it is recorded that at the end of his life, Jacob called Leah the head of his bed (his chief wife, the mother of most of his children).[1] So who was Leah?

The Bible paints Leah as the older, unattractive daughter of Laban. She never caught Jacob's eye, though he immediately and repeatedly expressed love for her younger and more attractive sister, Rachel.

The Bible has never recorded Jacob ever saying that he loved Leah, even after they were married. There is nothing mentioned of their commitment to each other and his desire to pursue her as a potential helpmate. For whatever reason, Leah just didn't attract Jacob's attention.

But that wasn't going to stop her father from marrying his unattractive daughter off to a potential suitor, even if it was through subterfuge.

As a result of these circumstances, Leah was victimized by the two most important men in her life, an opportunistic father who married her off deceptively, and then the man that she cunningly married who did not love her.

Some may say that Leah was a willing accomplice to the deception, because she could have spoken up when she was sent to Jacob if she did not want to participate in this trickery. But this may not be entirely true. During that era, fathers exercised all authority when making family decisions, especially when it came to their daughters, who were often considered second-class citizens. The power that the father had at home is nothing like now, where children can do whatever they want. Back then it was a different world. When your father said something, you immediately complied. He literally held your life in the palms of his hands.

Where was Leah going to go if she did not obey her father? Leah really did not have a whole lot of options, and so she did exactly what her father told her, thereby becoming the third and unloved point of a love triangle for the rest of her life.

Even today, when a woman is married to a man who does not love her, she often becomes nothing more than a pawn for his pleasure. You yourself may be or have been part of a love triangle, where you felt you were the unloved third point. While most likely you are not in a polygamous relationship, it is commonplace in our society for people to have extramarital relationships while they are married, believing that it's okay because these are "normal" occurrences. In modern times people make a marriage covenant to their partner at the altar before God and a host of witnesses, but don't fully commit to fulfill that promise. Regardless of its contemporary popularity, the love triangle always results in somebody coming out unloved, just like Leah.

At the end of the day, you may say, "I don't mind being in this love triangle because he loves me when he is with me." This is an unwise attitude toward your position. There is another side of this presumptuous relational triangle that is often disregarded: Somebody else may come along and replace you. Thus, it could be hazardous to your relational health to be involved in a love triangle, because you are looking for love in a place that has a revolving door. You are bound to this relationship at the will of the perpetrator. In the world of "anything goes," anything and everything can happen to you. You are not guaranteed the position of the "favored wife." Things change and people change—there is always a younger and more beautiful or handsome version out there somewhere. Unless God joins the two together in a covenant relationship and they keep Him first, you may be held captive to the will of your lover.

Leah got stuck in the perpetual circle of trying to be good enough to garner the love of a distant husband. Will you too allow yourself to get stuck in a fruitless relationship that renders you nothing but pain?

The choice is yours. Choose wisely.

chapter 2

THE REALITY OF LEAH'S UNLOVED CONDITION

Feelings of being unloved can be real and not a figment of someone's imagination...

I WANT TO SHARE A FEW THINGS ABOUT LEAH'S situation. First, the reality of her unloved condition was real.

When we are in situation of being unloved by others, we often try to downplay the gravity of it by saying things like, "God loves me," or "I don't need anyone else if I have God in my life." But do you know that being unloved is a very dangerous place to be in? As mentioned earlier, this situation can make you become replaced in the eyes of your spouse, a part of a love triangle that leaves you in a very lonely place. It is a place where, if we let ourselves admit it, none of us wants to be. If you truthfully revisit those times in your life, you will remember that isolated, dark feeling that left you feeling hopeless.

There are seasons in our lives where we often are rejected and disillusioned because love seems to have escaped us. If you are reading this book, there is a distinct possibility that you may be going through an unloved season in your life. You could be experiencing some of the most debilitating moments that you will ever go through in life.

On the other hand, maybe you're not the unloved one, but you know someone who is. You should be able to understand that Leah's pain was real when you read the Genesis account in the Bible. She was an unattractive woman, with a husband that really did not want her. She was tolerated but not desired. We should be able to understand that Leah's pain was real, as is the pain of those unloved ones around us, and not discredit it!

When we are counseling others who are saying that they are unloved, we often don't see the seriousness of their situation (sometimes, perhaps, because we don't recognize it in our own lives). Men, especially, don't often understand a woman's feeling of being unloved because they are wired differently. Sometimes, ladies, they can be really insensitive to the feelings of those who are unloved, dismissing it as a figment of their imagination. By nature men are problem-solvers, and they don't see the value of belaboring a subject. That's why they usually offer a suggestion with the expectancy that you will simply implement it, fix the problem, and move on. Jacob himself may have felt this way about his relationship with Leah.

Then there are the times when these individuals are approached with disdain, because their state of being unloved might be "contagious." Sometimes those of us who are counseling have the unrealistic and insensitive expectancy that somehow they are just going to snap out of it, saying things like, "You know *God* loves you, right?" If a woman comes to see you in tears because her husband does not love her, and you don't sympathize with the reality of her pain, you are being insensitive. The Bible wants us to know that being unloved is a reality for many in our society, and we should embrace them wholeheartedly and offer the love of Christ as a remedy.

Just because you are loved does not mean that those in your immediate, intimate circle are also loved. The Bible says in verse 31 of our passage that God *"saw that Leah was unloved"*; He was not only aware of the reality of her unloved condition, but also had recognition—full understanding and sympathy of—that condition. Leah in turn knew that God loved her, and yet she struggled with her feelings of being unloved by the most influential people in her life. Verse 31 indicates that God recognized the state of being unloved as a *condition*—it wasn't a fabrication of Leah's imagination, and it wasn't something that God said to "snap out" of.

God recognized her state as a condition… but what about the people in the Church? Sometimes we don't see the state of being unloved as an unbeneficial or harmful *real* condition, and we instead blame the person who has the problem of imagining things are worse than they are. However, if you are striving to be more like Christ, you cannot deliberately ignore the plight of someone who is unloved. God does not ignore them, and so you should not.

You see, God's plan for mankind on earth was for us to be loved not only by God but also by others. He didn't intend to bear that responsibility fully on His shoulders alone. If God had a plan for all of humanity to only be loved by Him, then He would not have created marriage!

Let me ask you: Can your mind comprehend the fact that you were not placed on this earth to be loved only by God?

It is theoretically true that the love of God is the most important thing in our lives; however, we were not created here to be loved only by God. We are wired to love and to be loved. It is okay for you to have a desire to be loved by someone other than God! He desires that you build godly relationships that mirror Christ's relationship with the Church.

In the same manner, God also commissioned you to be His arms extended to those who are unloved. 1 Peter 1:22 states, *"Since you have in obedience to the truth purified your souls for a sincere love of the brethren, fervently love one another from the heart."* God requires us to have the compassion of Christ when it comes to dealing with unloved brethren. He recognizes it as an unbeneficial condition in their lives, and He expects you to do something about it.

If you yourself are currently in a situation where you feel unloved, then prayer is one answer to your malady. You should be praying, saying, "God, I want to be loved with the God-kind of love that You preordained for my life." Understand that God may not send you the kind of love that you want, or He may not send you the kind of love that you thought was love. Yet I believe that for those who are unloved, when you cry out to God, He will send you love through human vessels.

We may have convinced ourselves that we don't need anyone to love us but God, simply because we are trying to cover our hidden shame of past sin, our current embarrassment, or self-depreciation. But those thoughts are distractive, disruptive, and contrary to the divine order of God. Being loved is part of that divine order, period. To those who say, "I don't need others to love me," it may sound spiritual, but it is not God's perfect will for your life.

Can you honestly say that God sent you here with all these people on this planet, and did not want anyone to love you but Him?

There are some people that have been unloved for so long that they have given up, and they cloak themselves in this lie. I don't want to get to that point in my life where I would say that I don't need anybody to love me but God, because I know deep down inside how much I *do* need someone to love me other than Him. There are people in nursing homes all over this country that have gotten to this point, saying, "I don't need anyone to love me but God." Why? Because their selfish children and family members don't go to visit them. These poor people have gotten to the point in their lives because there is no one there to make them believe any different.

The next time somebody asks you to pray for them, pray for them, because there is a yearning in every human being not just to love but to be loved. The reason we need to love our children, our husbands, our mothers, and our fathers is because it is part of God's mandate. There are no expendable people in our lives.

There are women who have been labeled "angry" because of their demeanor. That particular woman will often say that she's had a tough life and she has little to smile about, but she needs your love; don't let her tell you that she doesn't.

When a friend or coworker is in tears because her husband doesn't want her, she wants more than an "It's okay, God loves you." For some of us, that is about as deep as our spiritual vocabulary will go. It is *not* okay that someone is unloved! Do not tell anybody that. God is sending you to the rescue; if nobody else will love that person, you better start loving her, you better start sharing her load and caring for her.

Let me give a word to husbands, if you happen to be reading this: Men, the Bible mandates that we love our wives like Jesus loves the Church. Being loved is part of God's divine order. For those women that are in a season of being unloved by their husbands, it is one of the most difficult times in their lives.

There is one caution to this rule: If you are a man, and a woman comes to you saying that she is being unloved by her husband, you don't need to be the one loving her! And if you are the woman, you should not be going to men telling them that you feel unloved! There are some sharks in the tank at the Church that are just waiting for a sister to feel unloved so that they can take further advantage of her situation. They do not have God's purpose in mind, but only personal gain.

Know that God's only agenda is to fulfill His purpose and plan for your life. His Word says that absolutely nothing can separate you from His love. In Romans 8:38-39 Paul says:

> *For I am convinced that neither death nor life, nor angels, nor principalities, nor things present, nor things to come, nor powers, nor height, nor depth, nor any other created thing, will be able to separate us from the love of God, which is in Christ Jesus our Lord.*

When we envision Jesus on the cross, we see the love of God for each of us embodied in His ultimate sacrifice. God so loved *you* (make it personal!) that He sent His only son to save *you* and give *you* the gift of eternal life.

But...it didn't end there for you, and it didn't end there for Leah.

God did not leave Leah with the weak platitude of telling her that she was going to be okay. The Bible says that the Lord saw that Leah was unloved, stopped what He was doing, and then did something about it.

You see, some of us...we talk a good game, but, even though we know people that cannot get it done on their own, we fail to react with a proper response, a helping hand. You are missing so much in being a blessing to others!

You say that you went to college with her, she is important to you, and you used to hang out. She is going through a difficult season in her life, but she can't depend on you to lend more than a spiritual cliché. You know she is unloved, her marriage may be on the rocks—or she might not be married at all and is a single mom. You may know all that, and yet you don't even take the time to take her out for lunch, you don't even take the time to call her or send her a card or a text message to encourage her or pray with her. You don't do any of those things...

You may be a brother who knows another brother who is unloved by his wife. His wife is done with him, and he is in pain, but you don't want to encourage your brother because you don't want to get involved in their domestic relationship…

How is this being Christ-like?!

God needs the Church to provide an accurate response to the needs of those who have a broken heart and a contrite spirit. We *must* model God's reaction to the unloved condition of others, both in our own marriages and in our daily interaction with those hurting around us, if we are truly going to honor God and be the hands and feet of Christ.

chapter 3

LEAH'S RECOGNITION AND REACTION TO HER UNLOVED CONDITION

The thought that we don't need anyone to love us but God is disruptive and contrary to His divine order.

THE TEXT IN GENESIS IS VERY CLEAR ON God's response to Leah's unloved condition: God opened Leah's womb and blessed her with children.

Before we go further, let me stop right now and say one thing: For those of you that are not married, this doesn't apply to you at all. If you are unloved, God is not going to open your womb in order to heal you while you are unmarried. I always believe children are blessings from the Lord. Children are indeed a blessing for those of you who are unmarried and have one outside of wedlock, but the way you went about acquiring the child is a sin. What we are about to discuss is not applicable to those who are single; Leah was a *married* woman that God blessed because of her unloved condition. Single ladies, if "he doesn't put a ring on it," then God will use another means to show you His love.

Now, back to Leah. What Leah said at the birth of her first three sons was focused on her relationship with Jacob; what she said at the birth of her fourth son was focused on her relationship with God. Her comment after the birth of the fourth son, Judah, was the only comment that did not refer to her relationship with Jacob. Her sons were named after the things that she pondered on and desired in her heart. She wanted affection from Jacob when Reuben was born, an answer from God about her unloved dilemma when Simeon was born, an attachment to her husband when Levi was born, but only to give mere praise to God when Judah was born.

Let's examine each of these.

First, she desired *affection*. "*Surely the* LORD *hath looked upon my affliction; now therefore my husband will love me*" (Genesis 29:32). Leah longed for more of Jacob's affection, which Rachel had but she did not. Leah's lack of affection from Jacob really hurt her. She could not complain, however, because whether she willingly or unwillingly participated in the deception, she was a major contributor.

How often is it that when we use evil means to get something which we want very badly, when we get it we discover it has problems which can become great burdens to us. Many are those who have rebelled against God's way and will in marriage or in other matters obtain some coveted but forbidden possession only to have that possession become a real trial to them once they've got it.

Leah's words at the birth of Reuben expressed hope that Jacob would now give her more affection since she had given him a son, something every man wanted in those days (the name Reuben means "see a son"). Apparently, however, Jacob's attitude toward Leah remained virtually the same.

Because of this, she secretly desired an *answer*. *"Because the* LORD *hath heard that I was hated, He hath therefore given me this son also"* (Genesis 29:33). This is a play on words concerning the meaning of the name of this son, Simeon meaning "hearing" or "heard." The "heard" here indicates that Leah had prayed to God about this problem of lacking affection from her husband, and she believed God had answered her prayer. Simeon, therefore, represented an answer to prayer from God.

The lesson here is simple: When affliction comes upon us, even for our own poor behavior, we still need to take it to the Lord in prayer. We will find help when we pray. Of course, we need to note here that Leah should have prayed sooner—she should have prayed before she beguiled Jacob! It is good to pray at any time, but the necessity for many painful prayers of repentance could be eliminated if we were more prompt to pray beforehand.

Thirdly, Leah desired not just momentary affection from Jacob, but *attachment*. *"Now this time will my husband be joined unto me, because I have born him three sons"* (Genesis 29:34). The name Levi comes from a Hebrew root word which means "joined" or "attachment" and demonstrates Leah's hope that Jacob would now be joined in affection and commitment to her. Even after the birth of two sons, Jacob still was not giving Leah the affection or attention she desired, and she was still hoping for that relationship after she bore Jacob his third son.

It is instructive for the reader of Scripture to note the grace of God to Leah in giving her these three sons. The birth of her sons was the direct result of God's looking with sympathy on Leah's plight as the unloved wife (Genesis 29:31); He did not leave her without blessing. Yet, Leah tragically misapplied the blessings of God on her life. Instead of focusing on the blessing, her cry was still for that which she would not have: *"Now therefore my husband will love me...my husband [will] be joined unto me, because I have born him three sons..."* (Genesis 29:32–34).

The story presents a common tragedy of humankind. Leah was a victim; there is no disputing it. Born as "tender-eyed" and unattractive (Genesis 29:17), given to Jacob as wife in a fraudulent manner (29:23–25), and held captive in a marriage to a man who did not love her (29:30–31), she is one of life's unfortunate ones. When God changed her fortune with the birth of her sons, instead of taking comfort in

Him and His blessing to her, she rather hoped that the sons would change her previous victim status. This kind of attitude would only continue to keep her a victim.

It is a sad commentary on the human heart that we can be just like Leah. The acts of others may have put us into a situation that is unhappy, so our mindset is determined to somehow reverse our victim status. Leah wanted the love of Jacob so much, she could not appreciate the blessings of God. She attached a false meaning to the birth of her first three sons, clinging to a hope that could never be a reality.

When we have been victimized, it is counterproductive to hope that our status can be reversed. We cannot undo what has happened or redeem it ourselves. The better route is to look to God for *His* work to be accomplished in us. A love for God will allow us to make the correct applications to the events of our lives and know we are loved by God.

Bearing sons to Jacob did not win Jacob's love; instead, Leah was risking the possibility of coming to despise her sons when they inevitably failed to give her what she desired. It should cause us to wonder if we have sometimes despised blessing because we have attached the wrong outcome to it.

Eventually, though, Leah finally began to realize that part of the problem may have laid with her. By the time her fourth son was born, it seems she had undergone a change in attitude and focus. She now desired to *adore* Jehovah only.

"Now will I praise the LORD*,"* she said in Genesis 29:35. The name of Judah means "praise," and shows Leah's new focus. It is, amazingly, a most fitting name and pronouncement for the very son through whom Jesus Christ would descend. Leah, of course, did not know this about Judah, but her praising Jehovah was especially appropriate at his birth because of that fact. Whenever Jesus Christ comes on the scene, men need to praise God, for He is the greatest blessing man could ever have.

As we can see, Leah finally got her mind off herself and on to God when her fourth son was born. She opened her mouth and praised Him, and derived her comfort from *Him*, not her husband.

If we would praise God more, and complain less, we would decrease our miseries!

Eventually Leah came to accept her victim status, stopped trying to reverse it, and started making the right application of God's blessing to her life. *"And she conceived...bare a son: and she said, 'Now will I praise the Lord': therefore she called his name Judah; and left bearing"* (Genesis 29:35).

The apostle Paul wrote, *"...forgetting those things which are behind...I press toward the mark for the prize of the high calling of God in Christ Jesus"* (Philippians 3:13–14). Like him, like Leah, we must all seek to forget our perceived "victim" status and concentrate on present opportunities for obedience to God.

It is interesting to note that the Bible says God opened Leah's womb and blessed her with children, but also that He closed the womb of Rachel. God made sure that Jacob had to come and at least spend some time with Leah, because when the boys began to come, Jacob had a responsibility to raise them in the traditions of his people and prepare for his future legacy. So he had to begin to spend more time with their mother, Leah, whether he loved her or not.

Something eventually shifted in their relationship, apparently. Again, as Tamar Kadari states, *"Toward the end of his life, Jacob admits that Leah is the 'head of his bed' (the chief wife, the mother of most of his children)."*[2] Jacob also requested that he be buried next to Leah (Genesis 49:29-31) because of the virtuous woman she became once she surrendered to God's will for her life. He may not have ever loved Leah, but he at least came to respect her.

I believe that when God looks down from heaven and sees the unloved, He begins to mobilize a plan in order to bring love to that individual. In Leah's case, God's plan was for her to be blessed through children. Some of you reading this are single parents; have you truly realized what a real blessing you have in your children? They are the fruit of your womb. God gave the unloved matriarch Leah children to bring her joy and alleviate the pain in her life. Children are a blessing to their parents, from the Lord Himself.

I know it is difficult for some of you who are raising young children, changing diapers, and wiping snotty noses to believe this, but it's true.

I want to reemphasize that the biblical intent for bringing children into the midst of all your pain and suffering is to bring you the joy and love that you are missing. Children are taught to love and honor their parents their entire lives; it is what they are designed to do. As their parent, you are to train them to love and to honor you.

Single mothers, I've got some news that you may not want to hear, but that you need to hear nevertheless: You may never experience the love of a husband. God may be calling you to be single all the days of your life. You may live the next twenty years and never experience the love of a husband, and you have to be prepared for that. If God has promised you personally otherwise, then continue to stand in faith on His promise until it comes to fulfillment. You shouldn't have a defeated attitude and give up on marriage ever happening in your life, but you do need to prepare for that reality.

And use your time of singleness wisely. The time you spend hunting for your husband-to-be may be better spent preparing your children to be Godly men and woman who honor and love their mother. Some single mothers spend too much time looking for a husband, thinking in their mind that all will be instantaneously changed in their life if they could find someone to love them!

If this is you, you may see other women around you that have husbands and desire that more than anything, but you need to know and understand that God's love is an all-sufficient love. He is your El Shaddai, the All-Sufficient One. He has exactly what you need and is faithful to be all that you need Him to be in your life.

There are some women in this world that have gone from man to man to man, and, like Leah, have never ever experienced true love. Leah herself died without ever experiencing the romantic love only a husband can give. He didn't work seven years for her, he didn't do even the additional seven years of work Laban required for her—he did them for Rachel! On Leah's honeymoon night, when she offered her most prized possession to her husband, he had another woman on his mind. What depths of pain and misery she must have felt! Do you recognize a similar pattern in your own life? Is it really so hard to believe that these type of failed relationships between father and daughter and husband and wife combine so often and have become so commonplace for many of today's women? Often the problem starts at the age of fifteen or sixteen, or perhaps even earlier, when a woman gives her body away to someone who doesn't love her. Then it happens with a different man again and again but with the same results over and over. One day she finally does get married, and then the man she marries doesn't really love her either!

Single mothers, if you don't find the love of a husband, use your time to train your children. Why? Because these children can bring you the love, joy, and honor that a husband may not ever bring in your life. In America, we don't understand the importance of children. And if you are married, God expects you to have children. The bottom line is God commands us to be fruitful and multiply. Children are a great blessing to us, but we have to spend time nurturing them and teaching them to love and to honor us; if we don't, they won't! As Moses had to teach the children of Israel, so you will have to teach yours—that's why you need to discipline them.

Some important aspects to consider about raising children: Do not allow them to laugh at you when you make mistakes. It's not funny when your young children rebel. It is not cute. Demand that they respect you, and don't let them talk back to you in any kind of way; otherwise, when they get older, they won't honor you, and they won't bring you joy but pain instead.

You also cannot afford to not spend time with your children; they require a lot of your attention. My message to those who are unloved is to not further complicate your condition by neglecting your children. God opened Leah's womb so her children could be a blessing to her. You're setting yourself up to be dishonored when you ignore your responsibility to them.

Ladies, seeking a husband should not be your primary focus. You may have been to every club, every happy hour, and every church seeking him. But the question comes: "How is that working?" Your children, meanwhile, are your gift from God right in front of you; your priority is to love *them* now. In return, someday they will bring you great love, honor, and joy. Whether or not there is a man in your life, you need to begin to foster your relationship with your children and earn their respect.

I also want to take a moment and give a few words of advice to adolescents who are being raised in a single-parent home. Some kids who grow up in single-parent homes give their parents a lot of grief and pain. They dishonor their own name and that of their parents by disrespecting them. Their single-parent mother is up at night crying because she is lonely. She feels unloved and lonely, in addition to bearing the heavy responsibility of raising them on her own. With all the things she is going through, her children are at school not doing their homework, cutting up in school, hanging out with the wrong crowd, involved in all kinds of drug usage.

All they're doing is further complicating a difficult situation for their single-parent mom.

Their mouths are saying, "I love you, Mama; I love you, Mama," but they are lying; they are proving they don't love their mother by their actions. They are telling her "I love you" but bringing her nothing but grief. Shame on them!

The adolescent wouldn't want their mother just to say the words with her mouth with little or no corresponding action. She proves it by going to work every day, by keeping a roof over their heads, and by buying them the clothes they wear. They need to do the best they can so they bring a smile to her face. She doesn't need to be talking about going down to the jail to bail them out or see them with their hand held out all the time asking her for this or that. It is time for them to grow up and really show their mother that they love her.

Besides the blessing of children, there is also another provision God gives. Prayer is often an answer for those who have been rejected by someone they love. God clearly states in His Word that absolutely nothing can separate us from His love. His arms are always available, and His heart grieves when we are wounded by the selfish callousness of others. According to Isaiah 53, Christ Himself has born every major discomfort we will experience on the cross at Calvary and is now seated at the right hand of the Father, constantly interceding for us. So if you find yourself without hope because you are experiencing a broken heart, then find comfort in the knowledge that Jesus is praying for your restoration, and His love is always available and accessible to you.

As a Christian, being able to recognize the signs of someone who is unloved puts you in a better place to minister to those who are broken, rejected, and abused. An experience you can use to relate to that person empowers you to stand with them until you see a God-change take place in their life. It gives you an opportunity to help them experience the victory that you experienced when you became an overcomer in your situation. God takes everything in our lives and uses it for the good of His kingdom.

I know that right now that may be the farthest thing from your mind, but keep this notion close to your heart and remember that no matter what you are going through, God is there with you. He will see you through it until the end.

chapter 4

GOD'S VIEW OF UNLOVED LIFE IN THE WOMB

God's view is that life begins in the womb at conception.

GOD KNOWS US INTIMATELY BEFORE WE even show up on earth. As at the beginning of creation, God spoke the earth into being, and it was immediately formed by the Spirit of God. God also used the same method when He formed each earthly inhabitant.

Every master architect designs a blueprint of his creation before bringing out his tools to complete the job. That means that he must think about his creation and become intimately knowledgeable with his design. So was it with man. God said, *"Let Us make man in Our image."* There is further evidence in Psalm 139, written by King David, that God, the creator of all mankind, is intimately familiar with us before our mother's egg meets our father's sperm and conception takes place. Psalm 139:13–16 says:

For You formed my inward parts; You knitted me together in my mother's womb. I praise You, for I am fearfully and wonderfully made. Wonderful are Your works; my soul knows it very well. My frame was not hidden from You, when I was being made in secret, intricately woven in the depths of the earth. Your eyes saw my unformed substance; in Your book were written, every one of them, the days that were formed for me, when as yet there was none of them.

In this chapter we will be dealing with a lightning rod issue. In considering the topic of being unloved, we cannot ignore another people group besides women that is affected: the millions of children that are so unloved, they are not allowed into this world at all.

There are two very distinct worldviews about what exists inside a woman's womb after conception. One view is that the embryo is just tissue that can be discarded without any moral implications. The other is that the embryo is an unborn life that results in immoral consequences when discarded; those who align themselves with this worldview see this termination as homicide.

The overall message in this chapter is that the Church must not allow unloved children, both in and outside the womb, to be about politics. Both Democrats and Republicans will use this issue to advance their political agenda. Sometimes they do so without any genuine concern about the issue at all, one way or the other.

Democrats advocate socially saving lives outside the womb while they don't advocate saving lives of children in the womb. Republicans advocate morally saving lives inside the womb while they are not advocates for public assistance after the children leave the womb.

Republicans support legislation to let children be born because they consider abortion to be murder. But they also support the right to bear arms because you never know how people will act after they grow up. On the other hand, Democrats support legislation to stop children from being born at all because they are an "inconvenience," and most abortions are a matter of "convenience" for the parents of the child or their caregivers.

According to a 1998 study by Torres and Forrest (based on 1987 data), 21 percent of the women surveyed said that they had an abortion because of inadequate finances; another 21 percent said that they were not ready for the responsibility; 16 percent said that her life would be changed too much; and 12 percent said that there were problems with their relationships.

Abortion clinics are filled with women who say, "I'm not married, and I don't know about this man; he may leave me, so this baby's got to go, too," or "I'm too young and immature to raise a child," "My children are grown and I don't want anymore," or "I'm in the middle of building a great career; I don't have time to raise a child right now."

If we look at the issue *without the influence of public opinion*, the issue of abortion is merely about convenience; everything else is really a smokescreen. But there is only one view on when life begins that matters, and that is God's view. It doesn't matter what the Democrats, Republicans, or Independents say: as believers, if you say that you love God, that God is on the throne of your heart, that Jesus paid it all on the cross at Calvary, then whose view should be the only one that matters?

Some of us have been asked to agree with a lie for the sake of our political party. Let us not just acquiesce on this issue! We can't afford to do that, not on such a fateful issue. The body of Christ cannot allow itself to be used as a bargaining chip for votes, because we must have a Christ-centered view of life. The world, on the other hand, is not aligned to God and His Word.

This chapter is not designed for me to argue with you; I only want to leave you with a clearer understanding of what God's view is on this issue. What it comes down to is this: if you say you are a believer and that you love God, but God's thoughts and what God's Word says about this issue don't matter to you, then you have a much bigger problem that needs your immediate attention.

Every believer is required to seek God's truth in all things, but especially when it comes to any controversial situation. It doesn't matter how long you have erroneously believed what you have believed. It doesn't even matter what the problem is; if God addresses the subject in His Word, and His perspective is contrary to the current worldview, then we *must* change our minds to more closely mirror His. Sometimes I'll sit down and have conversations with my kids to check their spiritual temperatures. If they come up too hot or cold on the issue, I provide the biblical perspective with an expectancy that they will now do better because they know better. When it comes to issues that influence their spiritual outcome in life, I don't waiver on that expectancy. Frankly, I am not changing my mind—they've got to change theirs. And so it is with God our heavenly Father and us His children.

Not only must we consider the spiritual aspects of this issue, but also the practical side for us as Americans. 69 percent of pregnancies among Blacks are unintended, 54 percent among Hispanics, and 40 percent among Whites. This problem has very serious consequences for the African American community. Blacks comprise only 13 percent of the population, but account for 37 percent of all abortions done in the US;

black women are five times more likely to abort than white women. These statistics tell a very accurate story about the future of the Black community, and we are going to have to face the consequences of this issue.

So why don't we talk about abortion in the Church? Traditionally it has been somewhat taboo to do that—but why, when it is a very moral matter? We can't seem to have this conversation without political parties pressuring us into silence. But silence should not be an option when it comes to being God's voice on the earth; it is our mandate that we as believers mirror Christ not only in our lifestyle, but also in the decision-making process on issues that lend themselves to compromise in the body of Christ.

God's perspective on this matter should be more important to us as believers than the approval of man. We have a Christian and moral responsibility to know, understand, and promote God's agenda for life after conception. There are Pro-Life Democrats, those who say that they believe that life begins in the womb, but it's not the belief of the majority. That needs to be changed. We can start by beginning to set our agenda to align with that of God. If we are Christians, we should be able to have a perspective that doesn't oppose the Word of God—and compromising for the good of a political party should no longer be an option.

God's declaration of when life begins is clearly laid out for us in the story of Isaac and Rebekah and their twin boys. There's some interesting facts here, and hopefully they will reshape your viewpoint if it is erroneous, and give us all a new paradigm where we are reexamining the value of and saving lives from God's perspective.

Let's examine Genesis 25:21–24 then. The first verse says, *"Isaac prayed to the LORD on behalf of his wife, because she was barren, and the LORD answered him and Rebekah his wife conceived."*

For a woman to be barren means she could not produce life in her womb. When Isaac prayed on Rebekah's behalf, the Lord answered him and gave her the ability to conceive. That means that God placed *life* in her womb! This passage indicates, then, that God knows when a womb is barren, and He knows when a womb contains life. It wasn't until the Creator of all life answered Isaac's prayer that Rebekah conceived. God has more than a limited understanding of when life begins and ends; He is the only sovereign being that has the creative power to *create* life. It wasn't hard for Him to enable Isaac's wife to conceive because He is the source of all life.

The Scripture goes on to say:

> *But the children struggled together within her, and she said, "If it is so, why then am I this way?" So she went to inquire of the Lord. He said to her: "Two nations are in your womb, and two people will be separated from your body, and one people shall be stronger than the other, and the older shall serve the younger." When her days to be delivered were fulfilled, behold, there were twins in her womb.*

God has foreknowledge of the purpose of His creation because, after all, He is the Creator. Isaac and Rebekah knew Him as the Creator and petitioned Him based on that knowledge to bring forth life in a place that was fruitless or barren.

We see this again in Psalm 139. When he wrote about conception and development in the womb, David didn't have the luxury of the modern day scientific view of life…but God did. God designed the blueprint for what was going on in the womb, and now because of scientific modernization, we can see it too. We now have "proof" from what we can see about the human gestation period: life begins in the womb immediately after conception. There is no other view to be had.

Remember what Paul said in Romans 15:4: *"For whatever was written in earlier times was written for our instruction, so that through perseverance and the encouragement of the Scriptures we might have hope."* These Scriptures were all written for us and for our instruction today, even in twenty-first century America.

As American Christians, we have a unique challenge in our country in the form of "Population Control Centers." Did you know that Planned Parenthood drops 80 percent of their abortion-performing clinics into minority neighborhoods? Did you know that there are 36 million African Americans in America right now, and that since 1973, 16 million African American babies have been aborted? That means that almost 40 percent of the total Black population has been aborted! The African American population is on a steady decline, and researchers estimate that by the year 2038, Black political influence will be insignificant at best. There will not have enough blacks in the populace to warrant political representation in this great USA!

This is a crisis. We have allowed Planned Parenthood to come into our Black communities and convince young mothers that their babies are not viable human beings. Thousands of lives are being lost daily, and there are some middle class African Americans who have the attitude that, "Well, they are in the hood, they aren't going to make it anyway." If you have that attitude, you are a part of the problem, not the solution, and God is not pleased!

An article on the *History of Black Wealth in America*, submitted by the Mintel Group, Ltd., stated that, "Education and professional skills helped create the first generation of wealthy families in the mid-19th century, prior to and immediately after the Civil War." In other words, it wasn't long ago that we *all* lived in "the hood!" (The Urban Dictionary defines the word "hood" as "the ghetto.") If you an African American that's forty years old or older, you probably grew up in the hood somewhere. It might have been on the hot sweltering streets of the inner city or in one of those towns where you blink your eyes and you have traveled the full length of downtown, but you were in the hood.

I challenge you to consider: African Americans have not always been in a position to acquire wealth…but *you* turned out to be somebody. Why can't these babies be given a chance to live and turn out to be somebody, too?

Adults often look at their future the wrong way; they are concerned about the money it would take to raise these children. But those of us who "lived in the hood" didn't have a pot to cook in when we were growing up. You would share underwear with your siblings, you had one bathroom for everyone in the house, and you had one chicken to feed everybody at Sunday dinner and had to split the wing into three pieces. But all of us turned out all right. So why do we have an attitude that screams, "Those folk don't need to be having no babies!"?

It's because we've assimilated the posture of a nation committed to population control in urban communities, and don't see it for what it really is. Nobody's ringing the bell, but the population control must stop!

Historically, women have made the choice, of course. But, brothers, you have a parental responsibility too! My black brothers, whether young or old, why aren't you fighting for your rights as a parent? It doesn't matter if she's your wife or not, if it was a "mistake" or was caused by sexual sin on the part of two consenting individuals: when that girl is pregnant, when you tell her she needs to abort her baby, you are telling her to take the life of your son or your daughter! You too need to understand what God's view is about life in the womb after conception.

You see, the Bible is explicitly clear: *"You [God] wove me in my mother's womb"* (Psalm 139:13, emphasis mine). It is clear that life in the womb is God's creation. He chose mankind to have the important role of being a vessel in the conception and development stages of procreation. God could have chosen any vessel or process He wanted to bring life into the world, but He chose us as vessels and stewards of His creation. If God is who He says He is, He could have taken a rock and some sand and mixed them together and made us. But the Bible declares that God said, "No, I'm not going to do it that way. I'm going to bring children into the world through the womb of a woman."

It's God's plan, not ours; it is His creation. You may say it's your baby, yes; but it was God's baby first. It is His creation, you are a vessel; you're supposed to be a parent and raise your children, but your baby belongs to God.

How can we be advocates for the other things that God creates and not be advocating for the unborn child? The unborn child is often the most unloved person in our society today; if you feel that you are unloved, consider the life that is overlooked and snuffed out without even being given a first chance. How can we demand that we be loved by others if we don't even love those that God creates in the womb every day throughout our nation?

chapter 5

JACOB, YOU'RE GOING TO LOVE ME

"And I am tellin' you I'm not goin' / You're the best man I'll ever know / There's no way I can ever go / Darlin', there's no way No, no, no, no, way / I'm livin' without you... / You're gonna love me"[3]

IN AN EARLIER CHAPTER, WE IDENTIFIED THAT one of the great obstacles of being unloved is loss of personal stability.

I propose that Leah's story is probably one of the greatest tragedies in all of the Bible. Being unloved is a great tragedy for anyone and oftentimes when I read Leah's story, I get emotional just thinking about what was going on in her life and how she lived in such a loveless marriage.

As we read in Genesis 29:32–34, it seems that Leah reached the place where she made up in her mind that Jacob was going to love her no matter what. She said to herself, *"Jacob, you are going to love me."*

She reached a point in her life where she wanted Jacob to love her so badly that she was willing to do whatever it took. In verse 32 she said, "The Lord has seen my affliction," meaning that she believed God had showed her favor through childbirth because of her poor condition of being unloved by her husband. Because of this, though, Leah now assumed that she was walking in the favor of God, and that her bearing Jacob's children would make him love her.

This whole idea of walking in the favor of God is one of the most misunderstood things in present-day Christianity. Oftentimes, when people talk about walking in the favor of God, what they mean is that they expect everything in their lives to go well.

We find here that Leah was seen as walking in the favor of God, yet her husband Jacob *still* did not love her. So this shows us that God does *not* promise any of us that everything in our lives will always go all right if we just follow Him. That's not what He says at all. Have you noticed that Leah walked in the favor of God and was unloved, while Rachel did not walk in His favor and yet was loved by her husband? Not only that, but Rachel was also barren. Though she had the love of Jacob, she did not have the favor of God. How can this be?

Sometimes in this life, people that are not walking with God will still get things that those of us who are faithful to Him do not have. It's a fact. The Bible tells us that there will be those that will be wicked and ungodly, and that they will excel in this life.

But that doesn't mean that God does not love *you*. It doesn't mean that God doesn't have a plan for your life.

Why?

Because even if we do, God does not measure His love for us in what He buys for us or gives to us.

The Bible doesn't teach that. Leah *was* walking in the favor of God, and yet Jacob never loved her. In life, God's favor is not a guarantee that we will get what we want. There are plenty of times in our lives that even though we are not outside the will of God, things still don't happen exactly like we want them. There will be times in our lives when we are walking in the favor of God and we will get sick, and people will die, and we will lose jobs, and all manner of things will happen. That is all a part of the natural process of life.

But one of the things that we must all realize as believers is that even in the midst of every storm, God will always be there. That is, truly, what the favor of God is: *help in the midst of every trial and tribulation.*

Some of you measure God's love based upon how much money you have in your account or how well your family gets along or how successful you are. But I've got news for you: God loves you even if you've only got four pennies in your account.

You see, God's compassion and favor towards Leah did not captivate Jacob's heart to make him love her. Some people would think that Leah's walking in the favor of God would turn Jacob's heart to her…but it didn't. Sometimes we do things in the Church because we want to earn God's favor. We give money, we give things, we serve, we do this, we do that, and we think that walking in the favor of God will make this man or woman love us.

Leah was convinced in her heart of hearts that she could earn her husband's love because she had God's favor, so she said in her mind, "Jacob, you're going to love me." This created within Leah what I would call a "peace-less existence." Leah was restless because she could not make Jacob love her, no matter what she did. What woman doesn't want the love of her husband, especially after she has born him his coveted sons? The favor of God was extended to Leah through her ability to bear children, and yet she mistakenly thought that having sons would make Jacob love her, and therefore she had no peace. She was focused on her plan for happiness versus God's will for her life, and it rendered her "peaceless."

Some of us are living in a peaceless existence. Why? Because we somehow think that the things of this world are going to make better circumstances come about in our lives, instead of being thankful to the God of this world who really makes things turn around in our lives.

Leah was struggling, trying to make Jacob love her by having children for him. History reveals that it did not work, because it is impossible to force someone to love you! Do you know how many people in this world have tried to force people to love them? Some of you have kids, and you try to force your kids to love you by buying them stuff. You may have grown kids who are extremely dependent on you, and you think that if you just let them stay in the house, if you just give them money and pay their car note, they're going to love you.

What you don't understand is that you can't force a child to love you; you can't force a man, or a woman, or anybody else to love you. It cannot happen that way.

One of the great things about love is that love must be given *voluntarily*.

That's why I don't understand men who hit their wives or girlfriends, as if they can force them to love them back. You can't force your girlfriend or your wife to love you by striking her! She may pretend that she loves you because you put your hands on her, but you can't force her to *really* love you! It doesn't happen that way. You can get as mad as you want to, but you cannot force someone to love you. Someone will either love you or not because it is their *choice* to do so.

Leah was unable to find peace as long as she was trying to make Jacob love her. You know, there may be some of you ladies reading this book that don't have peace right now because you are trying to make a man love you. You're trying to make him love you by paying his car note, by buying him shoes and clothes, paying for his food, and paying for his bad habits. You might even pay for him to take his other girlfriend out. You are literally paying for everything! You have no peace in your life. Why? Because you're living your life for something impossible. You cannot force anyone to love you back. If he doesn't love you now, it won't matter what you give him—he's not going to love you based upon that kind of manipulative relationship.

Now let me take a moment and share something with the men who might be reading this. Men, you may have a good job and plenty of money and are trying to get Sister Sarah to love you. *Stop* right now! You might as well save your money because money can't buy her love!

Money might buy her time to hang out with you, or going out to dinner with you—it might even buy you a night of her time, but money is *not* going to buy her love.

So many people in this life have zero peace, because they're trying to force some folks to love them including their children. As we discussed earlier, there are some moms who have totally irresponsible kids that may say that they love their mom, but don't act like it. What those moms are doing by covering up their children's behavior is trying to win their love by allowing their disrespectful attitudes to continue.

Are you seeking "love" in all the wrong places? Never try to win someone's love by becoming their footstool. Never. People either love you or they don't, period.

What is the remedy for this? We must surrender ourselves to God's will for us, no matter what it is and no matter if we remain in the state of being unloved by others. It is when we pursue our own desires and selfish ambitions that we often leave the pathway of God's plan for our lives, thus rendering our lives void of peace. But if you belong to God and have surrendered your life to Him, then you are no longer your own. You've been bought with a price: the blood of Jesus. Until Leah completely surrendered her will to that of her Heavenly Father, her life was utter chaos.

You will find that the same will be for you. Either Jesus is Lord of your life, or He is not.

If He is, then you can rest assured that His plan for you is the best plan that you could ever have for your life.

If you want peace in your life, surrender your will to God and, like Leah found out, you will have that coveted peace that you so desperately desire.

chapter 6
LEAH FINDS PEACE

Even though we were created to love and be loved by others because God wants us to love one another, there will be times in your lives where love just seems so scarce.

You know, I'm not mad at Leah for trying to win Jacob's affections. A spouse is worth fighting for, even if there is only a remote possibility to start a loving relationship or rekindle the love that you once had. At some point, you loved each other, and you've been together for a while; recently you've been going through some tough times. If one of you comes to the conclusion that it's time to call it quits, then the other partner can't just walk away from the relationship without a fight. God expects you to put up some sort of a fight.

The bottom line is that you have been married all of these years, you've got kids together, and you've built a relational history. It's not time to quit, it's time to fall on your knees and ask

God what you can do to save your marriage.

Some of you walk away too fast. Sometimes people say things because they are just upset or mad. They get emotional and respond out of their hurt feelings. If my wife comes home and says to me, "I don't love you anymore," I'm not going to walk away; I'm going to fight to save my marriage. She's just confused or lonely or frustrated, but we formed a God-sanctioned covenant together until "death do us part." Some things in life are worth fighting for. It may not work out, you may lose, but at the end of the day you'll be able to say: "I fought a good fight!"

The Bible says, *"The enemy comes to kill, steal and destroy."* You might need to fight back and say, "Hey Devil, I'm not letting you kill my relationship, steal my marriage, or destroy my love for this woman or man. I'm coming right at you and all of your demons; it's time to throw down!" Every now and then, it is time to just tell the love of your life, "And I'm am telling you / I'm not going… / No, no, no, no way!" (Jennifer Holliday's song from *Dreamgirls*).

Your marriage is worth fighting for until the end. Christians run around fighting and believing for everything else. They will walk on the car dealership floor and put their hands on cars in a hot second, claiming, "This car is mine in the name of Jesus!" We've got Christians that will go rolling into jewelry stores and put a diamond ring on their finger and say, " Lord, you said, be specific! I claim that this six-carat pear-shaped diamond is mine in the name of Jesus!" We claim cars and houses and clothes and shoes; we claim everything! Then claim that your marriage will be healed! Claim your spouse back into right relationship with you and God. Claim *that* in Jesus's name!

Imagine Leah's struggle. She's wrestling in this state of peaceless existence, trying everything in her power to attract her husband's attention, putting on lingerie, making sure that everything in her household is perfect, and making sure she says the right things. She's living every day of her life for Jacob, and she has no peace.

But then finally in Genesis 29:35, she changes her chorus from "Jacob, you're going to love me" to "God, *You* will always love me." You see, the first three sons were all about Jacob; then the fourth son, Judah, comes and she realized, at that point, that God would always love her no matter what, and He deserved all of her praise for His unconditional love!

She began to understand after years of giving her best to her husband Jacob that even with God's favor, she could not win his heart. Reality set in with the birth of her fourth son, and she figured out that even her best was not enough to please Jacob. Leah changed after the birth of her Judah, whose name we know means "praise." She fully acknowledged *God's* love for her when she said, "This time I will praise the Lord!"

Leah finally got her mind on loving God only, which freed her to praise Him! You may be in a fight for your marriage right now, but don't ever forget that God always loves you. If your spouse never comes around to loving you, you must imitate Leah and recognize that *God* loves you. We have to realize that God will always love us. Again, Romans 8:38–39 is proof of God's devotion to us:

> *For I am convinced that neither death, nor life, nor angels, nor principalities, nor things present, nor things to come, nor*

> *powers, nor height, nor depth, nor any other created thing, will be able to separate us from the love of God, which is in Christ Jesus our Lord.*

They may not love you anymore, but God always will. Even though we were created to love and be loved by others because God wants us to love one another, there will be times in your lives where love just seems so scarce. During those moments, you must remember that God has not abandoned you, God has not left you; God is with you.

That is the ultimate peace we all search for.

chapter 7

GOD WILL ALWAYS LOVE ME

Peace came to Leah when God's love was more important than Jacob's love.

ONE OF THE GREATEST VERSES IN ALL THE Bible is John 3:16: *"For God so loved the world that He gave us His only begotten Son, that whosoever believe in Him shall not perish, but have everlasting life."* God loves us so much that He gave up His most precious gift so that we can have an eternal relationship with Him.

In His love for her, Leah found the key to change her state of "peace*less*ness" to that of peace*ful*ness. The transformation took her to an undeniable contentment, confidence, and assurance in her troubled life. She came to realize that God's love is really the only love that a person cannot live without. Her state of being unloved by her husband no longer tormented her; it no longer controlled her.

"Yadah" is one of the most explosive expressions of praise. It is a Hebrew word meaning to surrender in praise, and to throw out the hands in complete resignation to God, to give wholly in deference to God and total submission and adoration to Him. In fact, Leah was so resigned to her new state of mind that she named her fourth child "Yadah" (Judah)! Leah resolved, "Yes, I have these children. I'm in this bad marriage. I might feel like a single parent." But then she lifted her hands and said, "Yadah! I will praise the Lord."

A love that "feels" and does not "fill" is worthless. The love Leah could never feel, get, enjoy, or experience from a husband, God gave her through four sons, and a daughter shortly afterward. Jacob's love was based on pure feeling, but was not filling. Jacob might have satisfied Leah's sensual impulses, but he never surrendered his heart to her. A woman's romantic yearnings need to be satisfied, but Jacob never hinted that he loved Leah in any way. He never tried or wanted to love Leah. Instead, she received from her children and her God the love that Jacob never offered. This was a huge shift in her life.

For some of you, it's time for you to have this shift in your life too, and move into a state of peace with God's will for your life. You've been living in such peacelessness, that maybe you hate your job or you don't sleep at night. You're so stressed that you go to doctors and try to "diagnose" the problem. You don't have peace because you are trying to win the affection of your children, of a parent, of a spouse or a boyfriend. You spend all of your life trying to win the affection of people.

You don't want to live like this. You want to live in peace. The only way you do that is to say, "God, I want others to love me, I want my husband to love me, I want my wife to love me, I want my children to love me, I want my mother and father to love me, I want my friends to love me. I want that, God—You created me to be loved. But, *if it doesn't happen*, help me, God, to see that *You* fully and completely love me!"

Psalm 27:10 says, *"For my father and my mother have forsaken me, but the LORD will take me up."* You see, when everybody else forsakes you, then the Lord shows up! He will show up for you like He did with Leah!

The answer to Leah's unloved state was when

a *spiritual*—not circumstantial—shift happened in her life, something that changed Leah's focus: It was the love of God that commanded her attention! It pulled her out of the pain of Jacob's rejection into the loving arms of her God. There and only there did she find the peace that surpasses all understanding. He consoled her, He ministered to her, He showed her that He loved her…and she said *no more*! At last, she realized she had gone from being unloved by man to being *His beloved*.

Our God is not a respecter of persons. This kind of love is also available to *you*. This simple prayer from Psalm 108:5–6 holds the key to your peace: *"Be exalted, O God, above the heavens, and Your glory above all the earth. That Your beloved may be delivered, save with Your right hand, and answer me!"*

This is the heart cry that gets God's attention. This was Leah's cry, and God transformed her from peaceless to peaceful, from unloved to beloved.

He can and will do the same for you, if you would ask Him.

"MY BELOVED"

LEAH'S SONG OF PEACE

My heart rejoices in the love of my heavenly Father.
I am His always-and-forever-loving-daughter.
In Him there is no need for greed, He is my ever present help in time of need.
He has touched my life, and I am His indeed.
His favor surrounds me like a shield, and to Him, my life will I yield.
When I am lost in His loving embrace, my heart is no longer an empty place.
I am His beloved, and He is mine, because He alone will love me well until the end of time.

Endnotes

1. Kadari, Tamar. "Leah: Midrash and Aggadah." Jewish Women: A Comprehensive Historical Encyclopedia. 20 March 2009. Jewish Women's Archive. (Viewed on October 19, 2014) <http://jwa.org/encyclopedia/article/leah-midrash-and-aggadah>.

2. *Ibid.*

3. http://www.metrolyrics.com/and-i-am-telling-you-lyrics-jennifer-hudson.html

about the author

MICHAEL PENDER is the Founding Pastor of Fallbrook Church in Houston, Texas, where over four thousand families gather each week for worship and sound teaching. He was raised in the Bronx, New York, and moved to Houston in 1985, where he continued his education at Houston Baptist University.

Pastor Pender believes the greatest model for leadership is found in Jesus Christ and, therefore, believes in servant-leadership. He believes that his calling is to be a good shepherd over the sheep entrusted into his care at Fallbrook Church.

Pastor Pender is married to Janice Foreman Pender, and they are the proud parents of four children: Bailee, Michael Jr., Arnelle, and Colin.